EXPLORE
ANCIENT
WORLDS

THE
AZTECS

TAMRA ORR

Mitchell Lane
PUBLISHERS

P.O. Box 196
Hockessin, Delaware 19707
Visit us on the web: www.mitchelllane.com

EXPLORE ANCIENT WORLDS

Ancient Assyria • Ancient Athens
The Aztecs • Ancient Babylon
The Byzantine Empire • The Celts of the British Isles
Ancient China • Ancient Egypt
Ancient India/Maurya Empire • Ancient Sparta

ABOUT THE AUTHOR: Tamra Orr is a full time writer and author living in the Pacific Northwest with her husband and children. She is the author of more than 300 books for readers of all ages, including numerous titles for Mitchell Lane. A graduate of Ball State University, Orr loves exploring history and learning about ancient cultures and then sharing all she learned with her young adult children.

PUBLISHER'S NOTE: The facts on which the story in this book is based have been thoroughly researched. Documentation of such research can be found on page 45. While every possible effort has been made to ensure accuracy, the publisher will not assume liability for damages caused by inaccuracies in the data, and makes no warranty on the accuracy of the information contained herein.

Printing 1 2 3 4 5 6 7 8 9

**Library of Congress
Cataloging-in-Publication Data**
Orr, Tamra.
 The Aztecs / by Tamra Orr.
   p. cm. —(Explore ancient worlds)
 Includes bibliographical references and index.
 ISBN 978-1-61228-284-8 (library bound)
 1. Aztecs—Juvenile literature. I. Title.
 F1219.73.O77 2013
 972—dc23
                                        2012009411

eBook ISBN: 9781612283593

PLB

CONTENTS

Tenochtitlán, the Aztec capital

A Warrior in Training

Tototl shifted the heavy load of wood he was carrying. No matter how hard he tried, he could not find a position where the sticks did not dig deeply into the muscles of his back. With each step, the wood felt heavier and he felt even more eager to get back from the forest to the city, where he could put down his load and rest for a moment.

Although his arms and legs ached, Tototl smiled at the thought that carrying bigger loads meant that he had also earned a bigger meal. Even though it had been several years, he could still remember meals of only half a corn cake when he was younger. It had never been enough, but it taught him to accept hunger as a regular part of life. It was a lesson he knew would be valuable in his life as a warrior, the same as carrying heavy loads without a single complaint.

It was Tototl's first year at the *telpochcalli*. The school for the youth had already taught him many things. He closed his eyes and uttered a quiet prayer to Tlaltecuhtli, the goddess of the Earth, and Tonatiuh, god of the sun. He prayed for their guidance to find inner strength and courage, no matter what he would be asked to do one day in battle.

Although it had been months since Tototl started school, the day he was brought in front of the *telpochtlato,* the school's ruler, was as clear to him as if it had just happened. He could still hear the leader's voice as he spoke:

Here our lord has placed him. Here you understand, you are notified
that our lord has given a jewel, a precious feather, a child has arrived.
In your laps, in the cradle of your arms we place him. And now we dedicate
him to the lord, shadow, wind, Tezcatlipoca and pray that he will sustain him.
We leave him to become a young warrior. He will live here in the house of
penance where the eagle warrior and the jaguar warrior are born.[1]

That moment had been the best of his entire life! Tototl had been
imagining that day since he was very young and first realized he would
grow up to be one of the ruler's mighty soldiers. He loved being in the
school, but it was not an easy life. When the teachers were not working the
students' bodies, they were yelling, insulting and bullying the students'
minds. Tototl knew they did it for an important reason—to create tough,
powerful soldiers.

To help achieve that goal, every moment of each student's day was full
of chores and lessons. Tototl woke early, sometimes before the sun. After a
quick meal of corn cakes, he and the others were put to work. The day
passed slowly, as they swept floors, repaired canals and aqueducts, built
fences, and took care of many of the crops growing nearby. Hauling
firewood from the forest to the city was one of his least favorite chores, but
he could tell his muscles were stronger for the hard physical work.

Like everyone else, Tototl spent the rest of the daylight hours learning.
They were drilled in the use of a variety of weapons, from bows and arrows
to wooden clubs, darts, and shields. That part of the day went too quickly—
he loved finding faster, better ways to move and dodge. As he fought, he
pictured himself fighting an enemy and capturing prisoners to bring back
to his city. He felt his heartbeat speed up at the thought of his exciting
future.

Even so, there were times Tototl wanted nothing more than to ignore
the morning call for school. Instead of getting up and preparing for the
day, he wanted to roll over, shut his eyes, and go back to sleep. But he knew
what happened to students who were lazy or disobedient. Just last week,
the student Chimalli had been reported for not doing his share of the

A glimpse of the types of wooden spears, clubs, and arrows that comprised the weapons used by Aztec warriors in battle.

assigned chores. The priests—the school's primary teachers—quickly meted out a punishment. They pushed cactus needles into Chimalli's thighs, calves, and chest. Tototl winced at the thought and promised himself again that he would do whatever he was told, even if it meant exhaustion and sore muscles!

After Tototl dropped his load of firewood, he smiled because the sun was setting and his favorite time of day was ahead. Quickly, he joined the other students. They bathed, washing away the sweat and dirt of the day, and then dressed in loincloths, capes and neckbands.

Fires were lit and everyone gathered around them to sing, dance and listen to the stories of their gods and goddesses and tales about their bravest warriors until late into the night. Finally, the students returned to the school to sleep and let their minds and bodies rest before the day began again.

As Tototl lay down on his straw mat and pulled his small blanket over his shoulders, he stretched his arms and legs to relax them. Tomorrow he would get the chance to practice his weaponry skills in a mock battle with students from the *calmecac,* or school of the arts. In the darkness, Tototl

When Tototl and the other students sang and danced to honor their gods, it was easy to forget the hard work waiting for them the next morning.

Wooden drum (*teponaztli*)
Mixtec, AD 1200–1521

Horizontal drums were divided on top by slits into two tongues which emitted different tones when played with sticks bearing rubber tips. This drum is carved in the form of a supine captive who wears a turtle carapace armband. Vivid eyewitness accounts from the early 16th century tell of drumming ceremonies in which circling rings of dancers were ranked from the centre outwards.

Purchased by the Christy Fund Ethno. +6184

Drummer from Codex Becker
Mixtec, 15th century

Wooden drum (*teponaztli*)
Mixtec, AD 1200–1521

The complex scene carved on this drum is executed in the same style as the Mixtec painted histories. Five males and one female figure, armed with shields, are ritually opposed beneath the symbols of the Mesoamerican year sign and the sun god Tonatiuh. Each figure is associated with a place name and date.

Ethno. 1894,37.612

Wooden drum with owl image (*teponaztli*)
Aztec, AD 1300–1521

This drum is embellished with a low relief carving of a horned owl (*tecolotl*). As a creature of the night that nests in hidden recesses, the owl was perceived to be an emissary from the underworld. Drumming was used as a means of communicating with the realm of the dead and calling upon ancestral forces to intervene favourably when waging war.

Ethno. 1949.Am 22.218 (Oldman collection)

An Aztec drum from the British Museum

shook his head. The boys from that school were of noble birth and had been in school since they were very young. These students were taught differently with classes about the gods and goddesses, the calendar, the book of dreams, and how to use drums, reed flutes and bone rattles to make music. These students even went to school with girls, who were being taught how to become priestesses.

Because the *calmecac* students were the sons of the nobles, everyone knew the boys would become warriors—but Tototl knew he was a better fighter. He also knew that if he won tomorrow's mock battle, it meant extra food all day and perhaps even a small gift from the priests. Most of all, he knew his success would please and honor the gods.

The *calmecac* students would eventually become warriors, but their days were full of far different activities than those in the *telpochcalli*.

As Tototl drifted off to sleep, his thoughts turned to home. He missed his mother and father, as well as his younger brother Itzli and sister Teiuc, but knew he would see all of them soon.

In the dark, Tototl smiled to himself. He was one day closer to being out of school and on to an adventure where he knew he would be completely victorious. It was only a few years—and countless loads of firewood—away.

Time to Play!

Young Aztecs certainly worked hard, but they also enjoyed games. Just like today's top athletes are celebrities, the best Aztec athletes were honored and treated with great respect.

The Aztec game *ollama*

One of the most popular games was *ollama*, a ball game played on an I-shaped court with high walls. Players competed for points using a tough rubber ball that they tossed high in hopes that it would go through one of the two hoops hanging down in the court's center. The rest of the players fought as hard as possible to interfere. Scoring points required great aim and strength since the hoops were often 10 feet above the court and the opening was only about 12 inches wide. To make the game even more challenging, players were only allowed to use their hips, elbows and knees. It was very violent, and serious injuries were common. The best players were considered as valuable as the best warriors.

Another game unique to the Aztec culture was known as *volador*. Players put on costumes with beaks and feathers so that they resembled birds. They climbed a tall pole, from 60 to 90 feet high. They tied one end of a rope to the top and the other end around their waists. Then they would then jump off and spread their arms as if flying, in an ancient form of bungee jumping. They would sail around the pole until—hopefully—they safely reached the ground. The player who completed the trip the fastest and with the best style was declared the winner.

An Aztec village

Back at Home

Itzli put the heavy bucket of water down on the ground to stretch out each of his fingers. The half cake of maize he had eaten for breakfast was already becoming just a memory and he knew he would be ready for lunch long before it would be given to him.

He stood up straighter as his stomach grumbled. Hunger was part of training to be a warrior like his big brother Tototl, and he knew he could wait to eat. For now, he would hurry and get the water back to his mother and then return to the river to see if he could catch any fish. His day was full and already the sun was on its way up in the sky. He had fallen behind before and had been punished by his father. He was forced to sleep alone outside all night in a cold and muddy puddle. It had been awful, but at least he had not been forced to breathe the smoke of roasting chili peppers. He knew a young boy who had been held over such a fire! Itzli promised himself he would never go too slowly again.

"Here is the water," Itzli told his mother, as he walked into the kitchen. He set the bucket down with a sigh of relief, and just had time to smile at his sister Teiuc before he was back out under the hot sunshine on his way with nets and a harpoon to find some fish.

Fishing took time and patience, and it gave Itzli the chance to rest and think. As he held the net under the water, he spent a few moments thinking how long it would be before he could go to school like Tototl. At the age of eight, he was halfway there—but 15 still seemed like forever away.

He glanced down at his shadow on the ground and was sure it was longer than it had been before. Just a few days ago, he had undergone *Quinquechanaya,* the stretching and growing ceremony. He had been lifted by his forehead, and his fingers, hands, and arms—as well as his feet and legs—had been pulled on to encourage them to grow. His family had even pulled on his nose, ears, and neck![1] Itzli was sure the ceremony had helped him get taller. Now, he hoped it also would help him catch more fish.

When Itzli returned with fish, he found his mother and older sister Teiuc weaving cotton on the patio outside their house. They often spent the

hottest hours of the day out here where they could weave and still catch an occasional cool breeze. They sat on the ground on woven mats, talking as they spun. Itzli knew that the skirts and shirts they would make would be used later at the *tianquiztli,* or market, to trade for food or books made from paper of wild fig tree bark.[2]

His mother also made the loincloths that he and his father wore every day. Learning how to put the cloth over his right shoulder and tying it above his knee was one of the first things Itzli remembered learning when he was very young. Tying the loincloth below the knee was only for the nobles and anyone who forgot could be put to death! The nobles also added bright colors to their cotton, as well as feathers and jewelry, but Itzli's clothes were plain and simple. He liked it better that way.

Itzli was sure Teiuc was eager to head to the market, as it was often her favorite part of the day. He could understand that—the marketplace was such an exciting place, full of bright colors and endless sounds. Thousands of people shopped there every day for food, clothes and other goods. In one spot, someone might be getting a haircut, while next to him, a judge might be deciding who legally won an argument. Inspectors wandered through the stalls making sure no one was cheating, and doctors treated the sick or injured. Woodcarvers sold their work here, while stone and metal workers showed off their products as well. Many people sold their pottery along with griddles used for making tortillas. Traders came from other lands to show off their exotic wares. The marketplace truly was an exciting place to be!

Itzli sometimes joined the women when they went to the market so that he could see some of his friends. While his mother sold cloth from her stall, and Tieuc bought and traded with other vendors, Itzli collected any of the maize or beans that traders had left scattered across the floor. His father reminded him that helping out was a way in which he and his sister learned not to "spend their time in idleness, and to avoid the bad vices that idleness tends to bring."[3] It was another reminder that being lazy was almost as bad as being a coward and both would deeply disappoint the gods. Angry gods meant bad crops, defeat in battle—and great shame. Just the thought of

Children helping their mother store maize

those calamities was enough to terrify Itzli.

Inside Itzli's two-room house, smoke swirled in the afternoon sunlight. Without windows that would allow it to escape, the incense burning on the altar filled the small adobe house with a strong, sweet scent designed to please the gods. Ceramic jars painted in bright colors lined up against the wall, each one containing salt, ground maize and other ingredients for making meals over the open fire.

Itzli's mouth watered as he thought about the tortillas, tomatoes, peppers, and beans his mother made. He also loved the *atole,* or corn soup, his sister had learned to make for breakfast. It was sometimes spiced with peppers and other times sweetened with honey. Itzli looked forward to those special meals when meat was added to the recipes. He liked turkey the best.

Itzli went up to the flat roof of the house, briefly wondering what it would be like to have a second floor, even though only the nobles were allowed to build them. As he stepped out on the roof, he saw the beautiful flowers his mother had planted there and smiled. His home might be smaller and simpler than those of the nobility, but it was his favorite place in the world to be—at least until he was 15 and could start his education as an Aztec warrior, fighting for the gods.

Minding Your Aztec Manners

Almost everyone knows that good manners are important. To the Aztecs, they were much more than that—they were part of the law. Being polite and respectful was a rule Aztecs had to follow or else face severe consequences. Sometimes the punishment was a scolding. At other times, it might be physical torture or even death.

Some of the rules dictated who could wear clothes a certain way, while other laws focused on the importance of being a good role model. People were not to mock the elderly or the ill, nor were they to interrupt someone who was speaking or make faces.

Good manners were often taught to children at home. They focused on moderation, not doing anything to extremes. Children, even very young ones, were not to be too loud or too quiet, to walk energetically—but not overly so. They were to look directly at people, never past them or down at the ground. They were instructed to always wash after eating and clean up after themselves. Gossiping about other people was forbidden and one of the worst examples of rude behavior was public drunkenness. Punishment for this offense was often death! If people didn't like those rules, they couldn't say so. Complaining was also against the law!

Chalchiuhtlicue the Goddess
of Flowing Water

Women at Home, at Work and in Prayer

Tototl's mother Chimalma glanced up at the morning sky. Soon it would be time to put aside her weaving and return to cooking. She knew her family would be hungry—as always. She glanced over at Itzli as he carried the fish into the house. How fast he grew, she thought. She could still remember clearly the day he was born and the midwife took him outside to the courtyard and bathed him. In the traditional Aztec ceremony, the midwife touched him with water on the chest and head and gave him a drink, then prayed to the water god:

> My youngest one, my beloved youth . . . Enter, descend into the blue water, the
> yellow water . . . Approach thy mother Chalchiuhtlicue, Chalchiuhtlatonac! May
> she receive thee . . . May she cleanse thy heart; may she make it fine, good. May
> she give thee fine, good conduct![1]

This process introduced Chimalma's new son to the gods and helped name him. Itzli meant "obsidian," the name of the sharp stone used for cutting and carving. Tototl's name meant "bird" and Tieuc meant "second born." Each of her children had immediately grasped the items the midwife had handed them. Tototl's fingers wrapped tightly around the tiny shield, while Tieuc grabbed the small broom handle and Itzli had taken an arrow, proving he would one day be a great warrior like his older brother.

As she prepared the tortillas and beans for their midday meal, Chimalma was still thinking about those wonderful days when each of her children had been born. The gods had blessed their family to have three strong, healthy, wise children who knew their duties and did them without complaint. Punishment was rarely needed with any of them.

The midwife was an honored person in their world. She had taken care of Chimalma during each of her pregnancies. She had prepared her baths and massaged her tired body. She also gave Chimalma advice on what to

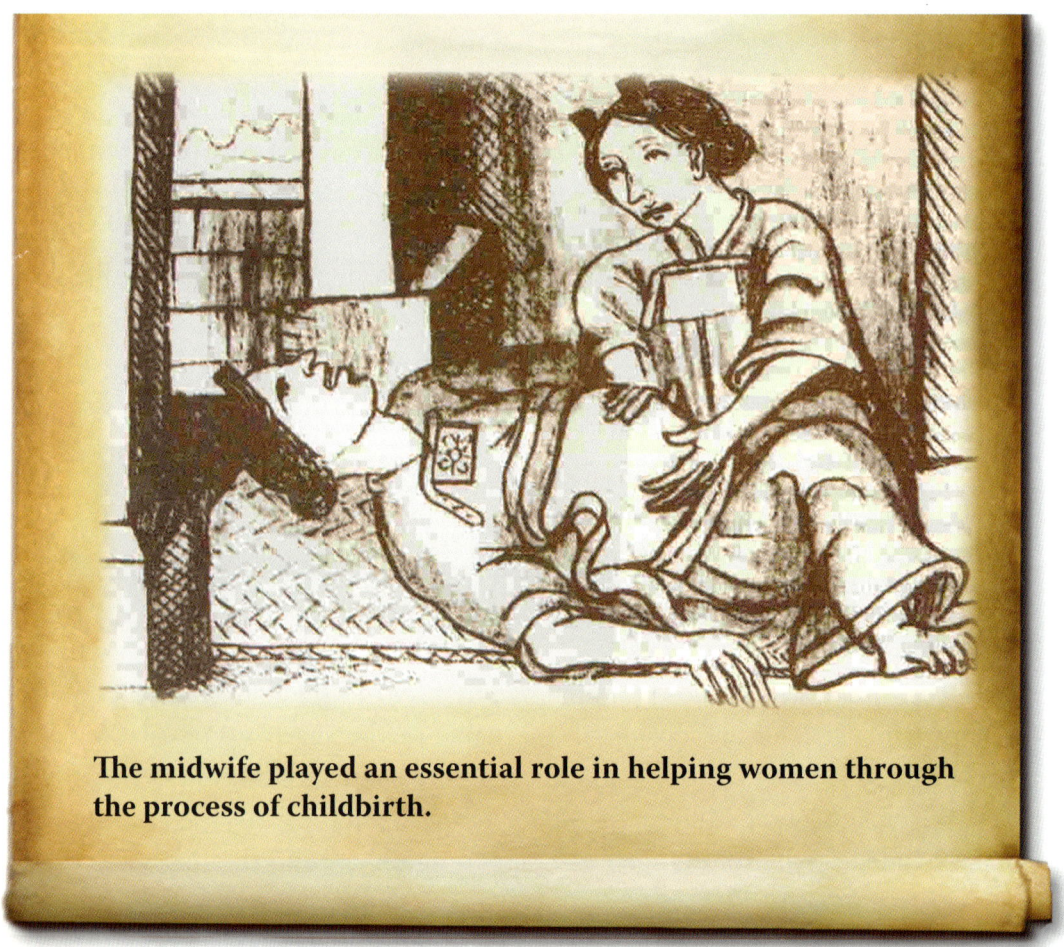

The midwife played an essential role in helping women through the process of childbirth.

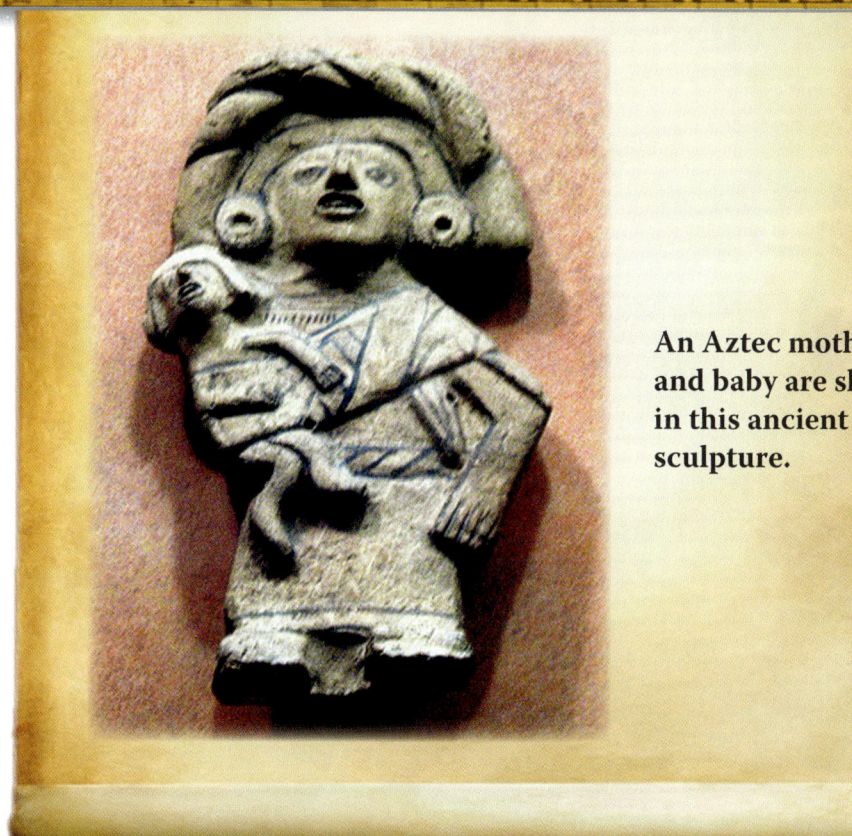

An Aztec mother and baby are shown in this ancient sculpture.

do and not do while pregnant. Chimalma smiled as she thought about how she had had to avoid looking at anything frightening or red and wasn't allowed to sleep during the day or walk at night. The midwife also helped Chimalma through each birth, and it was her responsibility to bathe and name each child four days later as the rest of the family watched. She always knew which herbs to use to help ease pain or speed up a labor that had slowed too soon. Often the midwife was also a healer and Chimalma was grateful for the help she had given their family over the years.

Chimalma listened to the sound of Tieuc singing outside as she wove the cotton fibers. Singing was a way to please the gods and it made her happy to hear the music flow so easily from her daughter. She so hoped that Tieuc would become a *cihuatlamacazqui,* or female priest. Since her daughter had been born, Chimalma had been taking incense and gifts to

Female priests were an important part of the Aztec culture. Here an Aztec woman is praying for a boy during the Day of the Dead celebrations in Mexico City.

the temple to show that Tieuc would enter the priesthood as soon as she was old enough.

It would not be an easy life for Tieuc, but a noble one. As a priestess, she would perform ceremonies, lead prayers, and sing songs designed to honor the gods. It would be her responsibility to read the calendar and interpret it for the nobles, as well as read horoscopes and help make sacrifices and offerings to the gods. Chimalma wondered if Tieuc would dedicate her life to the gods or end up marrying. Only the gods knew, of course.

Chimalma stopped working for a moment to gaze out the front door of her small home. She appreciated the cool breeze coming in and held out her *huipilli,* a loose white shirt that helped keep her cool in hot weather. Her hand briefly touched the simple necklace she wore, a strip of fiber with polished clay in the middle. She knew it was nothing like the gold and stone necklaces the nobles wore, but did not mind that it was against the law for her to do so. It was what the gods wanted.

Chimalma and her daughter did not wear makeup—that was for other types of women and not wives and mothers. Instead, she followed the advice her mother had given her as a child.

In the morning, wash your face, wash your hands, clean your mouth. Listen to me child, never make up your face nor paint it; never put red on your mouth to look beautiful. Make up and paint are things that light women use, shameless creatures. If you want your husband to love you, dress well, wash yourself, and wash your clothes.[2]

While she wanted her sons and daughter to have lives of grand importance and adventure, Chimalma was content with her own life at home. As she had been told as a very small child, "You must be in the house as the heart is in the body. You must be like ashes and the hearth."[3] She spent her day spinning cloth, sweeping the home, preparing food, grinding maize, tending crops and gardens, and teaching her children. She enjoyed talking with friends in the market and the process of bartering her

The temazcalli provided a hot, humid experience that helped people feel closer to their gods as they sweated out their fears and worries.

shirts, skirts and loincloths for the other items her family needed. She looked forward to the evening when she would go into the *temazcalli*, or "house of sweat" next to their home. Everyone in the family took a turn inside the little circular building. It gave them a chance to feel closer to their gods. Truly, Chimalma could not think how anyone—even the nobles—could possibly have a finer life than hers.

Garden in the Water

Many cultures have created unusual gardens of all shapes, sizes and even locations. The Aztecs were experts at creating gardens that floated on the surface of rivers, lakes and swamps. These gardens were called *chinampas*.

Chinampas seed beds

First, the people created straw raft-like mats. They planted willow trees in the corners of these floating gardens. The roots grew down and anchored the raft to the river or lake bottom. These trees also provided shade for the plants and were kept trimmed so they did not prevent sunlight from reaching the ground.

Next, dirt and mud were piled on top of the raft and then peppers, squash, corn, tomatoes and beans were planted. Canals were created in between the rows to water the plants, flowers and crops. Canoes passed through these canals so people could tend to the floating gardens. Fertile, rich, muddy soil was brought up from the bottom of these canals and added as fertilizer to the crops to help them grow.

Although some of these gardens were only five feet across and 50 feet long, the average *chinampa* measured 30 feet across and 300 feet long. In some cities, the floating gardens were responsible for growing as much as two-thirds of the food for the people's needs. Even today, some of these chinampas can be found in areas close to Mexico City. They support crops, as well as drawing tourists from around the world to see these amazing floating gardens.

Aztec temple

Among the Nobles

Far away from Chimalma's home, in the center of the city, was the palace where the emperor lived. The larger, fancier homes of the nobles and priests were nearby. In many ways, it was like a different world from where the commoners lived. The temples were also located here, sacred centers for the Aztec's many gods. Staircases ran up and down the sides of these immense structures, with a shrine and stone altars at the top. Tototl and his family had witnessed many sacrifices here. Some of the temples were shaped like pyramids, while others, like the one built to honor Quetzalcoatl, the god of the priests, were circular. The students of the *calmecac* who would soon battle with Tototl and his schoolmates of the *telpochcalli* went to school inside the temples.

The emperor was a powerful man who expected his people to follow him without reservation. His main job was to listen to and please the many Aztec gods. When he paraded through the city, he wore fancy embroidered clothes, shiny gold jewelry with gems and stones, and brightly colored feathers.[1] Tototl had been warned again and again to never actually look at the leader's face. It was not allowed. No one was to walk in front of him or make eye contact.[2] Most Aztecs were too frightened to even try. An upset emperor meant upset gods because they were in direct contact with each other. And upset gods meant everything from drought and famine to earthquakes and war.

The second in command was known as the *cihuacoatl,* or "snake woman." Despite the title, this position was actually filled by a male priest who dressed as the goddess. He was the emperor's main advisor, helping him make important decisions about rulings and the people. Below the snake woman were the *tetecutin,* or governors who wrote and interpreted laws, and *pipiltin,* the sons of nobility. They were military officers and served as priests.

The priests did far more than help with matters of religion. It was their job to lead the warriors into battle. They were powerful people and Itzli was equally fascinated and terrified by them. They often wore long black, hooded cloaks that went all the way to the ground. Many of these men had long hair, some of it so long it reached the floor. This hair was commonly

The ornate garb of the priests seen in this drawing shows the emphasis placed on them in the Aztec culture.

covered in blood from the many sacrifices they made on the temple altars to the gods.[3]

When Tototl and Itzli came to the city a year ago, they had been amazed at the size of the emperor's palace. It had more than 200 rooms in it. They were not allowed to go inside the palace, of course, but they walked around the outside and marveled at what they saw. There were many kinds of palaces and hundreds of them were stretched out across the Aztec region. Some, which were known as *tecpans,* were designed for the government to use and they had large courtyards. Other palaces were mansions where the nobles lived in luxury. Still others were retreats, beautiful resorts set up for the nobles to vacation and relax.

Tototl and his family would have been astonished if they could have seen through the palace walls to what was inside. Along with hundreds of rooms, it—as well as many of the mansions belonging to the nobility—included lush gardens, complete with fountains and canals to bring water to the flowers. One emperor was even known for having his own private zoo inside the palace courtyard. He had hundreds of birds, as well as monkeys, bears, and jaguars.

Jaguar

An Aztec noble is carried through the streets, illustrating the importance placed on them in the culture.

The meals served inside the palaces were far beyond the meager corn tortillas so many of the common people lived on. Hundreds of nobles were fed daily inside the palace, and meat was in almost every dish, including pheasant, partridge and even wild boar, as well as a variety of fish. Dessert often included a hot cacao drink that warmed the emperor and his nobles. Many leaders hosted banquets with hours of entertainment that included singing and dancing.

The lifestyle of the rich and powerful was very exciting and exotic to Tototl's family and other commoners. They honored the nobles as they also honored their gods. All young men, like Tototl, were expected to become warriors and fight for the emperor in his constant battle to conquer new lands and new people, as well as capture new sacrifices to send to their gods.

The World of Aztec Slaves

Aztec nobles had many slaves, who were primarily other Aztecs. How did a person become a slave? For some, it was the punishment for a crime they had committed. For many others, it was a way to pay off debts. Unlike the later situation in the United States, no one was forced to be a slave, nor could they be born into slavery. They were free to marry and could buy back their freedom. They could also earn their freedom one other way. If they

Aztec slave family

were on the way to the market to be resold and they got away and managed to run all the way to the palace without getting caught, they were immediately free. The only people allowed to chase the slaves were their owners—if anyone else tried, that person was punished by becoming a slave as well.

Lazy slaves were hard to punish—owners had to bring them to the plaza, and in front of other people, prove that their slaves were being disobedient. Once was not enough though. This process had to be repeated three times, and clearly demonstrate three instances of problems. Only then could the slave be sold to someone else. If a slave was resold to three different masters and turned back in each time, he was sold one more time—this time as a sacrifice to the gods!

Cortés meets Montezuma

The Aztecs at War!

Tototl's eyes flew open. He could not believe he had fallen asleep at all since he was so excited. Today was the day he had dreamt about for the past five years. Today he would go out into battle—a real one—for the very first time. He had trained for this exact moment—learned all of the moves, practiced how to wield the weapons and shield, and studied different ways to capture prisoners alive. He knew the key to pleasing the gods was the sacrifice of prisoners of war. Thousands of them had given their lives on the altars, their hearts plucked from their chests as people cheered. Many believed that if those blood sacrifices were not made, the sun would not rise the next day and the world would come to an end in a violent and terrifying earthquake because the gods were angry.

Now, at last, it was time to put all that Tototl had learned to use. He could barely contain his excitement. The emperor had ordered the warriors to battle the hundreds of invading Spanish soldiers and the school was buzzing with preparations.

In 1519, Spanish conquistador Hernán Cortés and several hundred Spanish soldiers came to Mexico in search of gold. Soon these men encountered the Aztecs. Emperor Montezuma II met Cortés and was shocked. This man, with his light skin and eyes and red hair, looked just like the Aztec god Quetzalcoatl. Stories had long been told of this god's return to earth—was this him? In case it was, Montezuma sent Cortés gifts and gold and welcomed him and his soldiers into Tenochtitlán. This turned out to be quite a mistake. Cortes wanted more gold, so he captured Montezuma and held him hostage in the city. Now, in the spring of 1520, the Aztecs—some of the strongest and fiercest warriors in the world—were ready to fight back. Tototl was one of them.

As he donned his feather helmet and salt-soaked, quilted clothing, Tototl uttered the prayer he had been saying each morning,

> There is nothing like death in war,
> Nothing like a flowery death
> So precious to Him Who Gives Us Life;
> I can see it far off. My heart yearns for it![1]

Tototl grabbed his fur and feather-covered shield. He knew that this battle would not be the same as others. Aztec warriors fought honorably and virtually never lost. Before they attacked a village, they warned the people, giving them the chance to give up and allow the Aztecs to take over. Up to 20 days were given to make the decision and then the village either surrendered and agreed to pay the emperor taxes, or the battle began. Groups of 200 to 400 warriors would approach, attacking in teams of 20 that were led by the priests.

This time, however, the war would work quite differently. The Spanish soldiers were not fighting fair. They had taken the Aztec leader by force and kept him a prisoner for several months. In addition, they had invaded the land and tried to steal gold from the Aztecs. Tototl was determined to help the warriors drive the Spanish back to where they came from. To battle!

The Spaniards tried to sneak out of Tenochtitlán. Tototl and his fellow warriors fought valiantly and killed hundreds of their enemies. They managed to drive the Spaniards out just as they had hoped. When they returned, they were greeted with roads lined with flowers, homes burning incense, and great rejoicing. Spanish prisoners were sacrificed on the altar and the many gods were appeased once more. The event became known to

The Spanish invasion of the Aztec empire in 1519 changed the Aztec's way of life.

the Spanish as "La Noche Triste," or "The Night of Sorrow" for all the soldiers that were lost in the battle.

Tragically, the victory was to be a brief one. In spring 1521, the Spaniards returned, this time reinforced with thousands of warriors from neighboring communities that the Aztecs had fought before and conquered. These communities had lost a number of their people to Aztec sacrifices and now they were ready to get revenge. They attacked the Aztecs every day, on foot and from boats. They also used a second, more silent weapon—smallpox and measles. These diseases killed more people than any of the battles. In addition, the Spaniards cut off all water and food supplies to Tenochtitlán, and destroyed the causeways that connected the islands to the mainland.

Within a matter of weeks, the Spaniards and their allies were completely victorious. On August 13, 1521, the last Aztec emperor, Cuauhtemoc, surrendered to Cortés and the capital city of Tenochtitlán fell. The Spaniards built Mexico City in its place and it did not take long before the entire Aztec culture had all but disappeared. One poet captured the heartbreak when he wrote,

After the arrival of the Spanish, along with their illnesses, the Aztec empire quickly came to a tragic end.

> Broken spears lie in the roads;
> we have torn our hair in our grief.
> The houses are roofless now, and their walls
> are red with blood.
> Worms are swarming in the streets and plazas,
> and the walls are splattered with gore . . .
> We have pounded our hands in despair
> against the adobe walls,
> for our inheritance, our city, is lost and dead.
> The shields of our warriors were its defense,
> but they could not save it.[2]

When Tototl had grabbed his shield and headed out to battle, he could not have known that the victory would not last. Within a few years, his entire culture would disappear. He only knew that he was a part of one of the best trained armies in the world and that using all he had learned on the battlefield was what he had been born to do. He was an Aztec warrior!

Home of the Prickly Pear

According to Aztec legend, the people came to find their land because Huitzopochitli, the god of sun and war, led them there. He had assured the Aztecs that one day they would have a place to call home, but they would have to watch carefully for the right signs to know when they had found it. According to Huitzopochitli, they were to watch for an eagle

Aztec eagle

perched on the top of a cactus. That wasn't all, however—the eagle was also supposed to be holding a snake in its beak.

Once the Aztecs spotted these three signs together, they were to settle down but—for once—not make war with the people living around them. Instead, the usually fierce Aztecs were to remain peaceful and focus on building a strong city that honored the gods. It took the Aztecs more than two centuries of traveling through the Valley of Mexico before they finally saw the signs. The legend states in 1325, a priest was on the shore of Lake Texcoco when he looked up and saw the eagle and snake atop the cactus on one its small islands. At last, they had found their home. They named the island Tenochtitlán, which means "place of the prickly pear cactus."

The Aztec Empire eventually covered more than 80,000 square miles between the Gulf of Mexico and the Pacific Ocean. Tenochtitlán became its center. At its peak, more than 300,000 people lived in Tenochtitlán.

Ancient Aztec Craft: Make Your Own Pyramid

The pyramids were very important to the Aztecs as religious temples, where they honored and made sacrifices to their gods. These structures took many years and countless workers to create, but you can make a miniature version quickly and easily.

MATERIALS
- 1 egg white
- Pinch of cream tartar
- 1 ½ cups confectioner's sugar
- Sugar cubes
- Pastry brush

DIRECTIONS
1. Beat together the egg white with the tartar to create a type of mortar or glue. Mix until soft peaks form.
2. Add the confectioner's sugar, one-quarter cup at a time until it is all combined.*
3. Create the base of the pyramid, using ten sugar cubes for each side.
4. With the pastry brush, cover these rows with the mortar you made.
5. Glue the rows together to form a square.
6. The second layer is made up of nine rows of nine sugar cubes each. Glue them together and then glue them on top of the base.
7. Add seven more layers, decreasing the length of the rows by one cube each time.
8. Put a single cube at the top of the pyramid.
9. If you want to make your pyramid look more authentic, consider painting it. You can also add sand around the base or whatever you like!

*Do not eat your pyramid—it may be made out of sugar but it also has raw egg in it, so it is not safe as a sweet snack.

Ancient Aztec Recipe: Spicy Chocolate Bark

Chocolate was a popular drink for the Aztec royalty and warriors. It was not much of a sweet treat, but more a spicy one served to help give warriors more energy for battle. Here is one way to make the kind of chocolate snack the ancient Aztecs would have enjoyed.

INGREDIENTS

½   cup hulled, unsalted pumpkin seeds
¼   teaspoon cayenne pepper
¾   teaspoon cinnamon
¾   teaspoon chili powder
12 oz. bitter or semi-sweet chocolate

DIRECTIONS (Be sure to have an adult's help when using the stove).

1. Put the pumpkin seeds in a skillet and toast over medium-low heat for about five minutes. As their inner oil is heated, they may pop and jump so be careful!
2. Look on the back of the chocolate package for specific directions about how to properly melt the chocolate. It should be done slowly and over low heat.
3. Once the chocolate is melted, add the cinnamon, cayenne pepper, chili powder, and almost all of the toasted pumpkin seeds.
4. Spread the mixture onto a flat baking pan lined with wax paper.
5. Sprinkle the top of the mix with the leftover pumpkin seeds, then sprinkle a little cinnamon, cayenne pepper, and chili powder on the top for decoration.
6. Place in the freezer for five minutes, or until the bark is completely hardened.
7. Break into pieces and serve—but keep a glass of water close by!

1100	Aztecs go in search of a new home to settle.
1195	Aztecs arrive in the Valley of Mexico.
1250	Aztecs settle near Lake Texcoco.
1325	Tenochtitlan is established and the first temple is built.
1350	Causeways are built with canals.
1375	Acamapichtli becomes the first Aztec ruler.
1395	Huitzilihuitzli becomes the second king of Tenochtitlan.
1417	The third king, Chimalpopoca, begins his reign, which ends when he is assassinated.
1427	Tenochtitlan's fourth king, Itzcoatl, begins his reign.
1431	Aztecs merge with Texcoco and Tlacopan to create the Triple Alliance.
1440	Moctezuma I begins his rule, which continues through 1469.
1452	Tenochtitlan is severely damaged by flooding, which leads to famine.

1469	Tenochtitlan's sixth king, Azayactl, begins his rule.
1481	Tizoc becomes the seventh king of Tenochtitlan.
1486	Ahuizotu succeeds Tizoc as king.
1487	The Aztecs expand into Mayan territories.
1492	Christopher Columbus lands in the Bahamas Islands, becoming the first European in what is known as the New World.
1502	Aztec Empire reaches its peak as Montezuma II becomes the ninth ruler.
1510	Tenochtitlan floods.
1519	Spanish explorer Hernan Cortés comes to Mexico and soon takes Montezuma as hostage.
1520	Aztecs drive Cortés and the Spaniards out of Tenochtitlan.
1521	Cortés returns with thousands of Indian allies and Tenochtitlan is destroyed.
1522	Tenochtitlan is rebuilt and renamed Mexico City, the capital of the newly established Spanish colony.

Chapter 1: An Aztec Warrior in Training

1. Manuel Aguilar-Moreno, *Life in the Aztec World* (New York: Oxford University Press, 2006), p. 99.

Chapter 2: Back at Home

1. "Instant Exercise: The Original Pull-Ups?" Aztecs at Mexicolore. http://www.mexicolore.co.uk/index.php?one=azt&two=fac&id=357&typ=reg
2. Michael E. Smith, "Life in the Provinces of the Aztec Empire." *Scientific American.* September 1997, pp. 76-83.
3. David Carrasco and Scott Sessions, *Daily Life of the Aztecs* (Santa Barbara, California: Greenwood Press, 2011), p. 107.

Chapter 3: Women at Home, at Work and in Prayer

1. David Carrasco and Scott Sessions, *Daily Life of the Aztecs.* (Santa Barbara, California: Greenwood Press, 2011), p. 99.
2. Jacques Soustelle, *The Daily Life of the Aztecs on the Eve of the Spanish Conquest* (London: Phoenix Press, 2002), p. 131.
3. A Woman's Journey: Women in Historic Aztec Society http://www.plu.edu/~mumperee/womans-journey/home.html

Chapter 4: Among the Nobles

1. Patricia Rieff Anawalt, "The Emperor's Cloak: Aztec Pomp, Toltec Circumstances." *American Antiquity,* Vol. 55, April 2, 1990, p. 291.
2. David Carrasco and Scott Sessions, *Daily Life of the Aztecs.* (Santa Barbara, California: Greenwood Press, 2011), p. 133.
3. Townsend, Richard F. *The Aztecs* (London: Thames and Hudson, 2005), p. 203.

Chapter 5: Aztecs at War!

1. Manuel Aguilar-Moreno, *Life in the Aztec World* (New York: Oxford University Press, 2006), p. 403.
2. David Carrasco and Scott Sessions, *Daily Life of the Aztecs* (Santa Barbara, California: Greenwood Press, 2011), p. 218.

Aguilar-Moreno, Manuel. *Life in the Aztec World.* New York: Oxford University Press, 2006.

Anawalt, Patricia Rieff. "The Emperor's Cloak: Aztec Pomp, Toltec Circumstances." *American Antiquity,* Vol. 55, April 2, 1990.

Anton, Ferdinand. *Women in Pre-Columbian America.* London: Abner Schram, 1973.

Carrasco, David and Scott Sessions. *Daily Life of the Aztecs.* Santa Barbara, California: Greenwood Press, 2011.

Evans, Susan Toby (editor). "Aztec Palaces and Other Elite Residential Architecture," in *Palaces of the Ancient New World.* Washington D.C.: Dumbarton Oaks Research Library and Collection, 2009.

Phillips, Charles. *The Illustrated Encyclopedia of the Aztec and Maya: The Definitive Chronicle of the Ancient Peoples of Central America and Mexico.* London: Lorenz Books, 2007.

Smith, Michael E. "Life in the Provinces of the Aztec Empire." *Scientific American,* September 1997, pp. 76-83. http://www.wcc.hawaii.edu/facstaff/dagrossa-p/articles/LifeInProvinces.pdf

Soustelle, Jacques. *The Daily Life of the Aztecs on the Eve of the Spanish Conquest.* London: Phoenix Press, 2002.

Townsend, Richard F. *The Aztecs.* London: Thames and Hudson, 2005.

A Woman's Journey: Women in Historic Aztec Society http://www.plu.edu/~mumperee/womans-journey/home.html

Books

Callery, Sean. *The Dark History of the Aztec Empire.* Tarrytown, New York: Benchmark Books, 2010.

Clint, Marc. *Aztec Warriors.* Minneapolis, Minnesota: Bellwether Media, 2011.

Heinrichs, Ann. *The Aztecs.* Tarrytown, New York: Benchmark Books, 2011.

Malam, John. *The Aztecs.* New York: M. Evans and Company, 2011.

Powell, Jillian. *The Gruesome Truth about the Aztecs.* New York: Windmill Books, 2011.

Raum, Elizabeth. *What did the Aztecs Do for Me?* Mankato, Minnesota: Raintree Books, 2011.

Schuman, Michael. *Maya and Aztec Mythology Rocks!* Berkeley Heights, New Jersey: Enslow Publishers, 2011.

On the Internet

The Ancient Aztecs

http://www.kidskonnect.com/subject-index/16-history/250-ancient-aztec.html

The Aztecs

http://www.kidspast.com/world-history/0281-aztecs.php

The Aztec Empire

http://www.pbs.org/conquistadors/cortes/cortes_a00.html

The Awesome Aztecs

http://aztecs.mrdonn.org/

appeased (uh-PEEZ)—Calmed or settled.

aqueducts (AW-kwuh-ducts)—Channels or canals to supply water.

conquistador (cahn-KWEES-tah-dohr)—Adventurer or conqueror; usually referring to 16th century Spaniards who came to the New World.

courtyard (KAWRT-yaard)—An open space in a building surrounded by walls.

debts (dehts)—Things owed to another person, often money.

drought (drawt)—A long period without precipitation.

famine (FAA-muhn)—Widespread, ongoing hunger.

harpoon (haar-POON)—Weapon similar to a spear, usually used to catch fish or other water creatures.

incense (IN-senss)—A substance burned for its smell.

inspectors (in-SPEK-tuhrs)—Official examiners.

labor (LAY-buhr)—The process of giving birth.

loincloths (LOYN-klawths)—Long strips of cloth worn around the legs and waist by Aztec men.

midwife (MID-wyf)—A woman who helped during pregnancy and childbirth.

mock (MAWK)—Mimic or imitation.

priestesses (PREES-tuh-suhs)—Female religious leaders.

smallpox (SMAWL-pawks)—An acute contagious viral disease.

tortilla (tawr-TEE-ya)—Flat Mexican bread.

vendors (VEHN-duhrr)—Sellers.

PHOTO CREDITS: All photos—CreativeCommons. Every effort has been made to locate all copyright holders of materials used in this book. Any errors or omissions will be corrected in future editions of the book.

47